GERMANY

GERMANY

MARTIN HÜRLIMANN

228 PICTURES IN PHOTOGRAVURE

8 COLOUR PLATES

INTRODUCTORY ESSAY

HISTORICAL NOTES

A STUDIO BOOK · THE VIKING PRESS
NEW YORK

ALL RIGHTS RESERVED
PRODUCED BY THAMES AND HUDSON LTD LONDON AND ATLANTIS VERLAG ZURICH
REVISED EDITION PUBLISHED IN 1961 BY THE VIKING PRESS, INC.
625 MADISON AVENUE NEW YORK 22, NEW YORK
LIBRARY OF CONGRESS CATALOG CARD NUMBER : 61-7448
PRINTED IN GREAT BRITAIN BY JARROLD AND SONS LTD NORWICH
GRAVURE PLATES PRINTED BY GEBR. FRETZ ZURICH
COLOUR PLATES PRINTED BY CONZETT UND HUBER ZURICH

GERMANY TODAY possesses no internationally recognized frontiers. If, then, author and publisher have seen fit to adopt those of 1937, this is not from any political bias but because it has seemed to them the only practical solution for a book which under the general title of 'Germany' sets out to present, above all, historic monuments and a cultural inheritance that goes back over a period of 1,000 years.

1 BACHARACH SEEN FROM THE RIGHT BANK OF THE RHINE

GERMANY

NO COUNTRY in Europe has had a more varied history than Germany yet none has preserved more traces of it in its landscape, its castles, its cottages and towns. From Bonn on the Rhine to Breslau on the Oder, from Hamburg in the north to Constance in the south the centuries have left imprints which even the Thirty Years War in the 17th or the thousand-bomber raids of the 20th century failed to erase.

The secret lies in the landscape, in the deep, impenetrable forests that imposed a clear pattern on Germany's development, even during the industrial revolution, and in the great rivers that formed both military barriers and arteries of trade. Standing on the outer rampart of the Saalburg, a modern reconstruction of a Roman fort above Frankfurt-am-Main, one can still see at a glance the chief ingredients of German history: the frontier-fortress, the rich medieval trade-centre below on the tributary of the Rhine, and the vast forested slopes of the Taunus Mountains that have played so great a part in German folklore and legend.

If any generalization can be made about a country with so complex a history as Germany, then it should be the contrast in development throughout the centuries between the Latinized lands of western and south-western Germany and the 'pagan' Germanic lands of north-eastern Germany. The German Franks who settled mostly in the valley of the Rhine with their chief capital at Frankfurt, were profoundly influenced by Roman culture, a fact which is still

II HEIDELBERG CASTLE

everywhere apparent. Later, in the Middle Ages, they broke up into a galaxy of independent States, bishoprics, and free cities. This was the area where Roman Catholicism gained its firmest footing in the Reformation and where the growing power of Prussia met with strong resistance. What many Germans would regard as the genuine German tradition, on the other hand, has its roots in the Saxon tribes that spread from the lowlands east of the Elbe over to Brandenburg and finally made Berlin their capital. Whereas the land in the west was broken up into small peasant holdings, the large Junker estates remained a feature of eastern Germany right up to 1945 when the Communists disrupted them. Strangely enough it was from the south, from the sun-warmed angle near Lake Constance, that the three dynasties came— the Hohenstaufen, the Habsburg, and the Hohenzollern—which were to bind these two conflicting elements together, under the aegis of Prussia, into one German State.

The Upper Rhine plain, which stretches northwards from Basel for over 150 miles to the beginning of the Rhine Gorge, is one of the most fertile and closely settled areas in Europe. To the west it is sheltered by the mountainous forests of the Vosges and the Hardt, to the east by the Black Forest and the Odenwald. Behind them lies the basin of the Main and the Neckar, much of it open arable land with such a clear pattern of orchards and vineyards as to be almost museum-like.

The pattern of settlement has remained roughly that of the early Germanic tribes, in the open, forest-free areas and along the rivers. Here too were the chief Roman settlements, which subsequently became the first bishoprics and medieval towns. There was a gradual thrust eastwards from Mainz and Frankfurt up the River Main, where the bishoprics of Würzburg and Bamberg were founded, and down the Danube where a succession of new towns were established, culminating in Vienna in the beginning of the 12th century.

It was with the development of trade routes in the Middle Ages, however, that Germany as a whole, and South Germany in particular, acquired most of its towns. By the year 1400 the country's present road and urban system was to a large extent complete. The industrial development some four centuries later made very little difference to the basic medieval pattern. Augsburg, Ulm, and Mainz, which were important medieval trading centres on the Transalpine route across the Brenner Pass; Regensburg and Nürnberg which became the commercial centres of Franconia; Frankfurt, Stuttgart, and Munich—all the sewere to expand far beyond their medieval confines to become major industrial cities.

In sharp contrast to the consistent economic and urban development of this south-western part of Germany, its political development has been extremely erratic, particularly in the Rhineland. Bavaria has always retained the shape of its medieval dukedom, but the whole region westwards to the Rhine became a mosaic of bishoprics, free cities, and imperial

domains. Constance is an old imperial city. Freiburg belonged for 400 years to Austria before it became part of the Grand Duchy of Baden. Speyer has eight kaisers buried in its vaults. Mainz was an immensely powerful archbishopric, which, together with Worms and Speyer, became absorbed in the Land of Hesse. With the advent of industrialization Mainz was superseded by Frankfurt, but it has remained one of the key cities in the Rhine-Main region. What was until fairly recent times a preponderantly agricultural population is today a hive of industry with a close network of roads and railways. Hanau produces jewellery, rubber, and cigars, Offenbach leather, Höchst and Ludwigshafen chemicals, and Frankfurt itself, in addition to being the hub of this great industrial wheel, is a centre of the engineering industry.

Although South-west Germany—Baden, Württemberg, Rhine-Palatinate, and Saar—has a great deal in common, both historically and economically, with the Rhine-Main region, it has for centuries been influenced by its association with Alsace and Lorraine, but more particularly in modern times when the exploitation of the Ruhr and Saar coalfields gave rise to the iron and steel of Lorraine. On the other hand, much of this area depends for its livelihood on domestic industries, principally textiles. But Baden and Württemberg have, of course, also become famous for their clocks and their musical instruments.

The Saar, which lies midway between Lorraine and the Rhine, is yet another area that typifies the changing political fortunes of these frontier-provinces and the fairly recent industrialization that was superimposed upon a preponderantly agricultural community. Confiscated by Napoleon from the House of Nassau, it then became a part of Prussia, was entrusted to the League of Nations under the Versailles Treaty, returned to Germany in 1935, came under French administration in 1945 and has only recently been the subject of a Franco-German agreement whereby it will be once again integrated in Germany but in such a way as to give France strong economic privileges.

The Lower Rhine valley, with important tributaries such as the Moselle and the Lahn, has always been one of Germany's richest areas. From very early times this has been a centre of wine-growing and commerce. From his capital in Aachen Charlemagne ruled the whole of Western and Central Europe. Towns like Cologne, Duisburg, Essen, and Dortmund were fully fledged cities 500 years and more before the invention of the steam-engine and the blast-furnace made the Rhine virtually an arm of the sea and turned the moors and farm-lands of the Ruhr into Germany's wealthiest industrial centre. Cologne, in fact, withstood the invasion of the machine-age until some fifty or sixty years ago. Today, unfortunately, little is left of the magnificent churches and medieval buildings that formed, up to the outbreak of the last war, the heart of the city.

The Münsterland, which lies north of the Ruhr district and stretches from the Dutch

IV LANDSBERG ON THE RIVER LECH

border to the Weser, has been comparatively unspoilt by industry, although the ancient town of Münster itself, with its university and its cathedral, has become an important railway centre. Essentially, however, the influence of the Rhine and the Ruhr is much less apparent. The towns of Münster, Paderborn, and Soest are on the invisible borderline between the Frankish and Roman Catholic culture from the west and the Saxon, later Protestant, penetration from the east. The frontier is crossed when one enters Niedersachsen.

Lower Saxony, which stretches along the northern fringe of the Harz Mountains from the Weser to the Elbe, is markedly different country from the Rhineland and Westphalia. Instead of church-villages and open market towns one finds great stretches of heath and moor with the old towns built round fortified cathedrals and feudal castles. Two conspicuous features are the Lower German dialect and the huge half-timbered farmsteads, in which living-quarters, stalls, stables, and barns are all assembled under one vast roof.

There are relatively small mineral resources; the main industrial districts are around Brunswick and Hanover. On the other hand, there is rich, closely populated agricultural land between the Weser and the Harz Mountains with small, historic towns that have changed little in the centuries.

Bremen, on the estuary of the Weser, and Hamburg, on the estuary of the Elbe, both built in the reclaimed marshes on the North Sea coast, have always led an existence independent of the province to which, geographically speaking, they belong. For centuries, since the Hanseatic League was set up with Lübeck at its head, both Hamburg and Bremen were independent States, enjoying enormous power and prosperity. Since then they have expanded —and more particularly Hamburg—both as ports and as centres of population. Unhappily Hamburg, like Cologne, suffered heavy damage during the last war, much of it in the old parts of the city.

Under the Carolingians the Elbe and its tributary the Saale formed the eastern frontier of the Reich, dividing Germans from Slavs, and a feature of this region are the fortress towns like Meissen and Torgau, many of which also became important trading centres. As on the western border, the historical pattern is extremely varied, but one important fact stands out: it was in these frontier-provinces that the foundations of Prussia and Saxony were laid.

Central Germany, which covers the whole of the Middle Elbe basin across to the German-Czechoslovak frontier, is densely populated and highly industrialized. Economically speaking, it stretches over into Bohemia. Five great cities dominate it, all of them with roots deep in the Middle Ages: Leipzig and Dresden, both famous cultural as well as industrial centres, Chemnitz, Magdeburg, and Halle. But there are also vast areas of rich arable land, particularly in the north between Leipzig and Magdeburg. It is, in fact, a characteristic of heavy industry in Saxony, as against Rhineland-Westphalia, that plants are few and very large and make, in

v WANGEN IN THE ALLGÄU

consequence, comparatively little inroad into the agricultural land. The industrial population lives, for the most part, in modern settlements or in the suburbs of small medieval towns such as Wittenberg. The main artery for this entire region is the Elbe with Magdeburg, lying half-way between Hanover and Berlin, acting—till the Iron Curtain dropped across Germany—as a key point in the communications from west to east.

The Baltic provinces to the north and the north-east offer a complete contrast in more ways than one. The entire strip of provinces—Schleswig-Holstein, Mecklenburg, Pomerania, and East Prussia—is predominantly agricultural and thinly populated with very few large towns. The landscape near the coast is not unlike East Anglia, rolling, arable country backed by wooded hills. Mecklenburg in particular was till recently an area of large estates, while Schleswig-Holstein was part of the area of original German settlement west of the Elbe and its dialect and domestic architecture have obvious affinities with Lower Saxony. But east of Kiel is medieval colonized land, where the Slavs were subdued in the 12th century and the first of North Germany's colonial towns, Lübeck, was founded. Other ports soon followed, mostly to the east of Lübeck and all members of the Hanseatic League.

The conquest and Christianization of the Lower Vistula and East Prussia was left to the Teutonic Order of Knights, who transferred their headquarters from Venice to Marienburg, then to Königsberg, where, 250 years later, the first King of Prussia was to be crowned. The Polish influence persisted, however, after the downfall of the Teutonic Order till Poland was partitioned at the end of the eighteenth century. Meanwhile the power of the Hansa had declined and Lübeck, like Hamburg and other independent cities, was ultimately absorbed into Prussia.

The nucleus of the modern State of Prussia was Brandenburg, which began as a frontier-province on the west bank of the Lower Elbe, then expanded east towards the Oder, moving its capital in the same direction from Tangermünde on the Elbe to Brandenburg and finally to Berlin. The real growth of Berlin, however, took place comparatively recently, in the 17th and 18th centuries, under the Hohenzollerns.

The city was built round the old town centre of Berlin and the neighbouring village of Kölln; it also embraced the Court district of Dorotheenstadt and Friedrichstadt. This sub-sequently became the business, shopping, and administration centre, which was virtually razed to the ground in the Second World War. Greater Berlin reaches out to the old towns of Spandau and Potsdam in the west and Köpenick in the south-west, all three today in the Soviet Zone. Within a considerable radius there are small towns, like Kotbus and Forst to the south, which became minor industrial centres as a result of migration from Berlin and which, although they have built up a much wider clientele, still market their produce in the

VI TÜBINGEN

capital. Others, like the ancient town of Wittenberg, where Martin Luther nailed his famous protest to the church door, have developed along more independent lines thanks to local resources of raw materials and labour.

Berlin's chief rival, Munich, though in size only Germany's fourth city, is the ancient and modern capital of Bavaria with a Roman Catholic tradition as pronounced as the Protestantism of Berlin. Bavaria's industrial production lies elsewhere, in the ancient cities of Nürnberg, Würzburg, and Bamberg. But, like Munich, their industrial development did not blur the medieval pattern or encroach too far on the surrounding countryside. The great plateau around Munich and the lakes and mountains to the south, the wooded hills and valleys in the Nürnberg area, and the fertile Main valley in which Würzburg is situated offer as much variety and beauty as any part of the German landscape.

It is difficult to find any single *leitmotiv* in this German pattern, which is, in fact, a pattern of Germanies. For Germany is still, as Metternich once said of Italy, largely a geographical expression. The Frisians on the North Sea have the slow, laconic speech that is typical of monotonous landscapes, while those in the Rhine-Main region, the country of Goethe, are essentially mobile and affable. Thuringia is associated with flowers and music and the mysticism of Luther, while the land east of the Elbe still bears the marks of colonization. Germany is a country that has produced radicalism and conservatism, poverty and wealth: a land of contrasts and of immense possibilities.

STEWART THOMSON

VII INTERIOR OF THE MONASTERY CHURCH, OTTOBEUREN

THE PLATES

ICHENAU, MITTELZELL 1

NEUBIRNAU

ERLINGEN 3

TERUHLDINGEN 4

HOHENZOLLERN

HEGAU

MEERSBURG

ST. MÄRGEN

HWARZWALDHAUS 12

GLASHÜTTEN, SCHWARZWALD 13

RASTATT

EMMENDINGEN

BREISACH AM RHEIN

TÜBINGEN, HÖLDERLINTURM

LUDWIGSBURG, SCHLOSS 21

STUTTGART 22

STUTTGART

STUTTGART, HAUPTBAHNHOF

NAGOLD

SPEYER, DOM-KRYPTA

WORMS, DOM

MICHELSTADT

VIERZEHNHEILIGEN

WEINBERGE BEI WÜRZBURG

WÜRZBURG, KELLER JULIUSSPITAL

BAMBERG, DOM

WIESBADEN

ASSFURT AM MAIN

ROTHENBURG OB DER TAUBER

ROTHENBURG OB DER TAUBER

MAINZ, DOM

FRANKFURT AM MAIN, RÖMER 45

FRANKFURT AM MAIN, DOM

BRAUBACH, MARKSBURG

CAUB

LORELEY

BORNHOFEN, BURG LIEBESTEIN, STERNBERG

52

OBERWESEL

BACHARACH

ST. GOARSHAUSEN

TRIER, DOM

TRIER, PORTA NIGRA

LIMBURG AN DER LAHN, DOM

WETZLAR

ALSFELD, RATHAUS

BONN, MÜNSTER

KÖLN, ST. COLUMBA

DÜSSELDORF, MARX-HAUS

SIEGEN IN WESTFALEN

ALTENPLATHOW

RHEIN-HERNE-KANAL

ZECHE GERMANIA/DORTMUND

SOEST

XANTEN

MÜNSTER

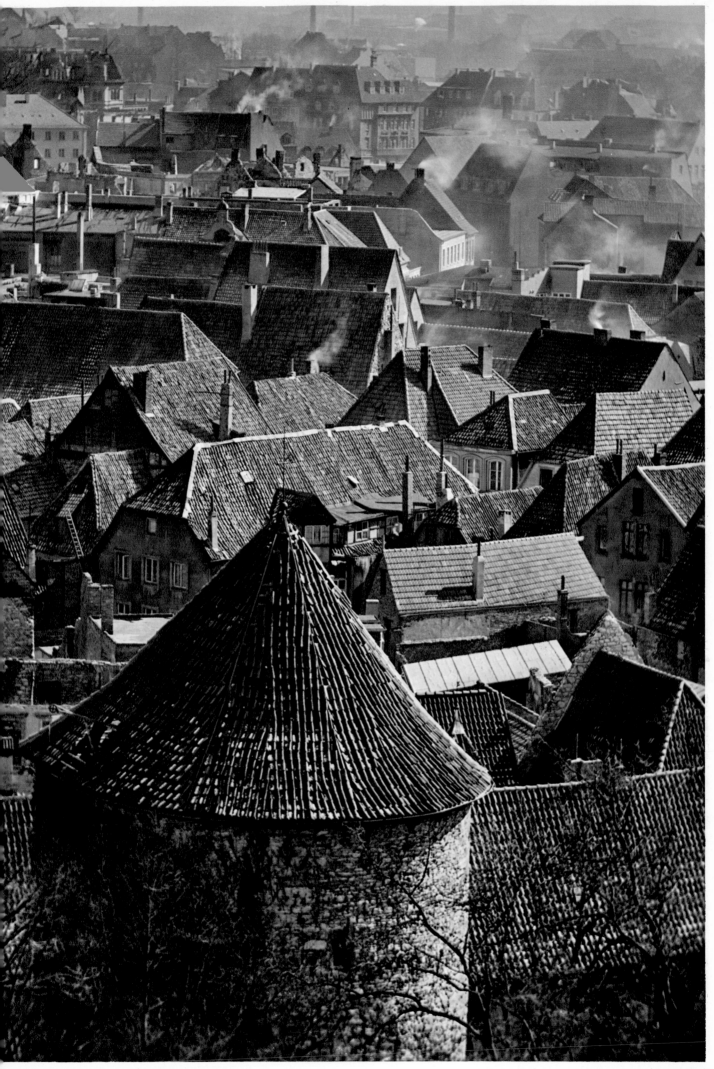

SCHLOSS GEMEN

OSTFRIESLAND

FEHNSIEDLUNG, OSTFRIESLAND

LMGO, RATHAUS

BREMEN, BÖTTCHERSTRASSE

OSTFRIESLAND

VEGESACK, WESER

KASSEL

HILDESHEIM

BROCKEN, HARZ

GOSLAR

EDLINBURG, STIFTSKIRCHE

WOLFSBURG, VOLKSWAGENWERK

HANNOVER, HERRENHAUSEN

HEIDEHOF BEI CELLE

BRAUNSCHWEIG

TANGERMÜNDE

MAGDEBURG. DOM

NEBURGER HEIDE

HAMBURG

STADE

HALLIG HOOGE

KOOGE, NORDFRIESLAND

FLENSBURG

LÜBECK, HOLSTENTOR

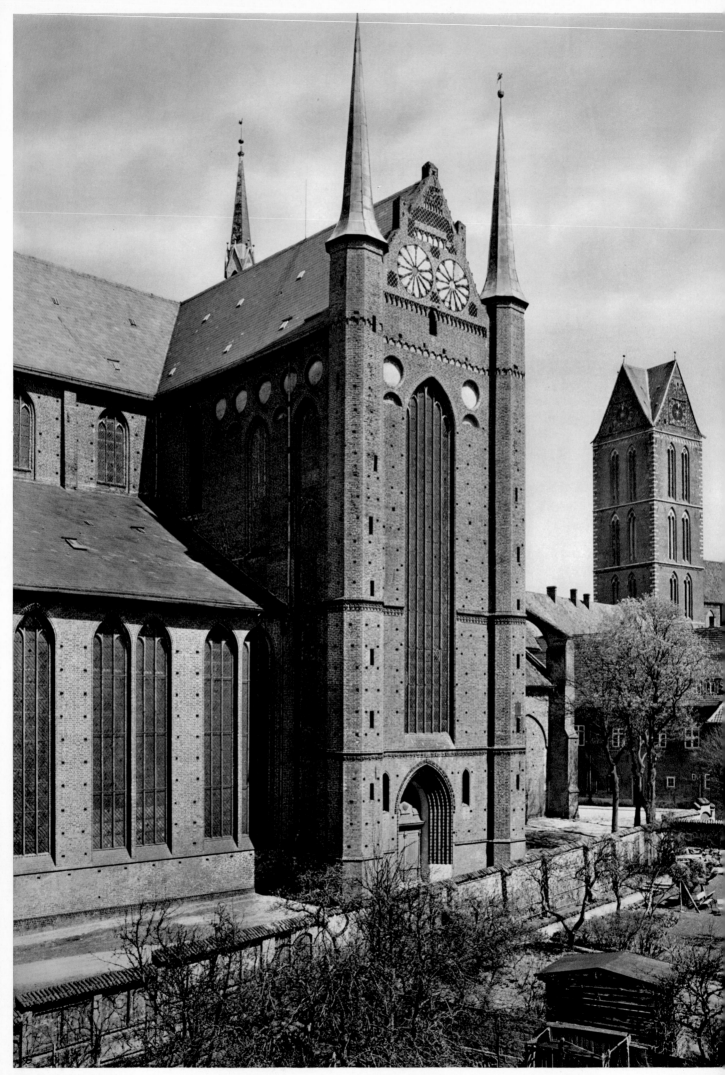

WISMAR, ST. GEORG

VELBERG, DOM

HAVELLAND

MÜGGELBERGE

BERLIN, SCHLOSS CHARLOTTENBURG

BERLIN, BRANDENBURGER TOR 136

BERLIN, STALINALLEE 137

BERLIN, KONGRESSHALLE

BERLIN, HANSAVIERTEL

BERLIN, ZEUGHAUS

CAROLINE FRIEDERIKE
VON HUMBOLDT
GEBORENE
VON DACHEROEDEN
GEB DEN XXIII FEBRUAR
MDCCLXVI
GEST. DEN XXVI MAERZ
MDCCCXXIX

FRIEDRICH CHRISTIAN
CARL FERDINAND
WILHELM VON HUMBOLDT
GEB DEN XXII JUNI
MDCCLXVII
GEST. DEN VIII APRIL
MDCCCXXXV

GABRIELLE VON BÜLOW
GEB VON HUMBOLDT

ALEXANDER
VON HUMBOLDT
GEB DEN XIV SEPTEMBER MDCCLXIX
GEST DEN VI MAI MDCCCLIX

POTSDAM, SANSSOUCI

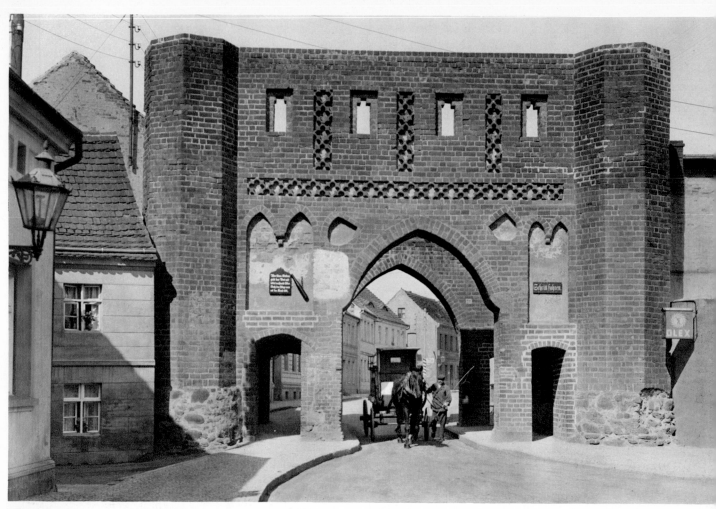

JÜTERBOG

ZINNA

BRANDENBURG

MARIENBURG

HEILSBERG

DANZIG

ERZGEBIRGE

SPREEWALD

FRANKFURT AN DER ODER, RATHAUS

BAUTZEN, ORTENBURG

ODER BEI MALTSCH

GÖRLITZ

GÖRLITZ

SCHLESIEN, WEBERSTUBE

JOSEPHINENHÜTTE, RIESENGEBIRGE

RÖMBERG, WEBERHÄUSER

OBERSCHLESIEN

LEIPZIG, THOMASKIRCHE

170

DRESDEN, ZWINGER

DRESDEN, HOFKIRCHE

MORITZBURG

MEISSEN

WÖRLITZ, SCHLOSSPARK

ERFURT, DOM

1

EISLEBEN, LUTHERHAUS

EISENACH, BACHHAUS

VESTE KOBURG

JENA

WEIMAR, GOETHES GARTENHAUS

WEIMAR, FRAUENPLAN

WEIMAR, MAHNMAL BUCHENWALD

OSSWEINSTEIN, WIESENT-TAL 191

RCHHEIM 192

NÜRNBERG, PRELLERHAUS

BAYREUTH

ANSBACH

WILLIBALDSBURG BEI EICHSTÄTT

ELLINGEN

WOLFRAMSESCHENBACH

DINKELSBÜHL

NÖRDLINGEN

NÖRDLINGEN

MERKENDORF

LAUINGEN

KLOSTER BEURON

WIBLINGEN

SIGMARINGEN

WASSERBURG AM INN

REGENSBURG

REGENSBURG

AUGSBURG, FUGGEREI

MÜNCHEN, DEUTSCHES MUSEUM

MÜNCHEN, WITTELSBACHER BRUNNEN

NYMPHENBURG

SCHLEISSHEIM

HENSCHWANGAU

ETTAL

WAGENBRÜCHSEE

OBERBAYERN

NIGSSEE, ST. BARTHOLOMÄ

SEEALPSEE, ALLGÄU

HISTORICAL NOTES

I BACHARACH seen from the right bank of the Rhine. Above the town is the Stahleck palsgrave castle (which has been turned into a Youth Centre), and at the foot of the castle hill are the ruins of the Werner Chapel. The other towers belong to the medieval fortifications of the town (see also Plates 54–5), To its right the tower of the municipal Church of St Peter (13th century).

II View across the old Neckar bridge towards HEIDEL-BERG CASTLE, which, although it has been in ruins for several centuries, still gives a unique impression of the magnificent way in which the beauty-loving electors of the Palatine displayed their taste in architecture. They transformed the medieval castle into a palace, the individual buildings of which no longer possessed any defensive purpose. The picture shows the Frederick building (rebuilt at the beginning of the 17th century) and on the right the English building, which was put up by the Elector Frederick V, the 'Winter King'. At the foot of the castle lies the town with its famous university and important industrial installations.

III LEER in East Friesland on the River Leda not far from the place where it joins the River Ems. With its little harbour and brick-built houses, Leer has the appearance almost of a Dutch town. The beautiful house in the middle of the picture, which dates from the 18th century, could easily be on the other side of the near-by frontier. The building with the tower is modern.

IV LANDSBERG on the River Lech. The Baier Gate of 1425 with its sculptures and outworks flanked by little towers. It was usual in the Middle Ages to decorate town gates with Christian symbols or figures although none is as well preserved as this gate at Landsberg. The town has been Bavarian since 1268, and was of importance as a trading centre and for its custom-house.

V WANGEN in the Allgäu. View along the main street towards the 17th-century Ravensburg Gate, which is a specimen of the medieval city gate clothed in the form of Early Baroque. Wangen was an imperial city until 1802. It retains a number of stately houses, several 18th-century fountains, and a number of excellent examples of wrought-iron inn signs.

VI TÜBINGEN. View of the collegiate Church of St George, which dates from the 15th century and in the chancel of which is the memorial vault of the dukes of Württemberg (see Plate 20).

VII OTTOBEUREN. View from the intersection of nave and transept towards the high altar of the monastery church, which is one of the chief works not only of the master-builder of churches, Johann Michael Fischer, but of all church architecture of the 18th century. It was begun in 1737; it was under Fischer's direction from 1744, and it was completed in 1766 (see Plate 224).

VIII Hansa Quarter, BERLIN (cf. Plate 139). One of the skyscrapers designed by the architect Hans Schwippert, Düsseldorf, on the occasion of the International Building Exhibition in 1957.

Photogravure Plates

-4 LAKE CONSTANCE lies in the basin of the large Ice Age Rhine glacier. Its shores, which are divided between Switzerland, Germany, and Austria, contain some of the oldest monuments of Central European culture.

1 The fertile island of REICHENAU, in the southern arm of the lake (Untersee) contains the ruins of some very ancient monasteries: Oberzell (St George), Mittelzell (St Mark), and Unterzell (SS. Peter and Paul) which were of European importance in Ottonian times (manuscript illumination and chased work). The monastery church of Mittelzell is here seen from the north-east, showing the choir, transept, and west tower. (Chancel 15th century, nave and west sections 11th century.) Emperor Charles III (d. 888) is buried here.

2 The pilgrims' church of NEU-BIRNAU on Lake Constance, the most southerly of the magnificent

Swabian Baroque churches. It was built by Peter Thumb 1747–9. The decorations were carried out by J. A. Feuchtmayer and his assistants. Neu-Birnau was the summer residence of the prelates of the near-by Cistercian monastery of Salem.

3 View southwards from the shore of LAKE CON-STANCE near Überlingen across the Bodanrück to the Swiss shore. In the background the massif of the Säntis.

4 UNTERUHLDINGEN near Meersburg. Recon-structed lake-dwellings of the later Stone Age.

5 Like the old imperial castle of the Hohenstaufen, the castle of the HOHENZOLLERN, which is also mentioned in documents as early as the 9th century, stands on a mountain at the edge of the Swabian Jura. The old castle was almost completely destroyed in 1423 and rebuilt in 1493. In the 19th century it was restored by order of Frederick William IV.

6 The HEGAU comprises the area between the Randen, the Swabian Alb, and Lake Constance. Several extinct volcanoes from the Tertiary Age give the landscape its characteristic appearance.

7 The castle, situated on a rock overlooking the little town of MEERSBURG on Lake Constance, was probably built in the 7th century. In 1211 it came into the possession of the bishops of Constance, who took up official residence in it in 1526. From 1835 until 1855 it belonged to the Freiherr von Lassberg. Annette von Droste-Hülshoff, the poetess, spent her last years here (1841–8).

8 The 'Hemdglonker' procession in MEERSBURG, a local custom in the district around Lake Constance. It takes place on Maundy Thursday, the so-called 'schmutzigen Dunschtig' (Schmutz: fat, grease— because of the cakes baked at Shrovetide, and Dunschtig=Donnerstag: Thursday).

9 The Benedictine monastery of ST BLASIUS was the most important of the many early monasteries founded in the Black Forest. After a fire in 1768 the church was rebuilt by d'Ixnard. The rotunda is one of the few church buildings in French classical style

erected on German soil. Today St Blasien is a mountain health resort, particularly frequented by those with lung diseases.

10 The *concilium*, or merchants' house, by the harbour at CONSTANCE. Constance, a settlement reaching back into prehistoric times situated at the point where the Rhine flows out of the main part of the lake into the Untersee, became the seat of a bishopric, later transferred to Freiburg i. Br., in the 6th century, a Free Imperial city in 1192, and developed into an im-portant trading centre during the Middle Ages. The great Church Council of 1414–18 convened in the merchants' house, which had been completed in 1388. Here, in 1415, the Hohenzollerns were invested with the fief of the March of Brandenburg and Johannes Hus burnt as a heretic.

11–13 THE BLACK FOREST, its southerly portion built up of gneiss and granite, its northerly covered with coloured sandstone, falls steeply down in the west to the valley of the Upper Rhine. In the east it descends gradually to the layered countryside of Swabia.

11 ST MÄRGEN. Interior of the monastery and pilgrims' church on August 15, Ascension Day (Kräuter-büscheltag). The present building is the reconstruction (made in 1907) of a Baroque structure which goes back to a foundation of the 12th century. To the left of the picture peasant women in their holiday cos-tume, of a type that is still met with today in the upper reaches of the Black Forest.

12 PEASANT HOUSE by the Schluchsee. The com-bination (under one roof) of living quarters and stabling is typical of these generally isolated Black Forest farmsteads. The roof slopes steeply in order to give protection against the snow in winter.

13 The Black Forest village of ALTGLASHÜTTEN.

14 RASTATT. Market-place with monumental fountain and the 18th-century church. From 1705 to 1770 Rastatt was the seat of the margraves of Baden, and town and castle were built to a uniform plan commis-sioned by Margrave Ludwig Wilhelm, known as 'Turkish Ludwig'. The Treaty of Rastatt in 1714 ended the War of the Spanish Succession.

15 Town gate at EMMENDINGEN, the former capital of the County of Hochberg.

16 FREIBURG IM BREISGAU. View of the minster from the Schlossberg. Like the Swiss Freiburg in Üechtland, Freiburg i. Br. was founded about 1091 by the dukes of Zähringen. In 1368 it came into Austrian possession, and was incorporated in Baden in 1806. Its university was founded in 1457, and in 1821 the town became the seat of an archbishopric. The minster is built of red sandstone and its earliest parts reach back to the 13th century. The tower (377 feet high) was completed in the 14th century and was a model for the whole of Europe in the Middle Ages. To the left of the tower the Church of St Martin in whose monastery Berthold Schwarz is said to have discovered gunpowder. In the background the Kaiserstuhel, the ruins of a long-extinct volcano.

17 BREISACH on the Rhine. View of the MINSTER of St Stephen from the west. The town lies above the river on a basalt rock. Its position in a frontier area has determined its turbulent fate which led to its almost complete destruction in 1945. The main parts of the minster date from the beginning of the 13th century. The projected large west tower, begun early in the 14th century, was never completed.

18 BADEN-BADEN. View of the monastery church. The town, which is magnificently situated between slopes of the northern Black Forest, was frequented as early as Roman times for its healing springs. Until 1706 it was the seat of the 'upper margravate' of Baden. From the beginning of the 19th century onwards it developed into one of the most elegant spas in Germany.

19 The Cistercian Abbey of MAULBRONN, founded in 1146, is the best preserved medieval monastic building in Germany. From 1558 onwards the monastery housed an evangelical school, attended by Johannes Kepler (1586-9) and Hölderlin (1786). The garden in front of the church together with parts of the cloisters and the refectory is one of the most important examples of Late Hohenstaufen planning (about 1230).

20 TÜBINGEN. View across the Neckar towards the Hölderlin Tower, the home of the poet during his long illness (1806-43). After its university, founded in 1477, the town's most important landmark is the Protestant Chapter in the St Augustine monastery, visited by Hegel, Schelling, and Hölderlin among others.

21 The castle at LUDWIGSBURG, garden façade. It was built in 1704-33 by Nette, Frisoni, and others for Duke Eberhard Ludwig, and was used by the dukes of Württemberg as alternative residence to Stuttgart.

22-4 STUTTGART (population 570,000), which has been the capital of the State and Province of Württemberg since 1482, developed in the 19th century into one of the most active industrial and commercial centres of Germany. Modern architectural style, in which Stuttgart early had important achievements to its credit, has given the town its characteristic appearance.

22 Aerial photograph of the centre of the old town with the castle and cathedral.

23 View of the whole town, situated in a branch valley of the Neckar.

24 The main STATION by Paul Bonatz (begun 1914, finished 1928) was the first modern solution to this constructional task and served as an international model with its smoke-free platform approach.

25 In the small town of MARBACH (Württemberg) on the Neckar stands the timber-framed house in which Friedrich Schiller was born to Kaspar Schiller, an army surgeon, and Dorothea Kodweiss, a baker's daughter. The family lived here until 1763.

26 NAGOLD on the River Nagold. Typical half-timbered house with the magnificent old inn sign 'Zur Post'.

27 Heavy industry in the SAAR. The Saar has had the typical fate of a frontier area. By language it is German. From 1381 it belonged predominantly to the House of Nassau, was French from 1793 to 1815 and then Prussian. Under the Treaty of Versailles it received a League of Nations administration, but in 1935 became a part of Germany again. In 1945 it came under French administration which was

replaced in 1947 by a parliamentary régime. From 1957 the Saar has been a part of the Federal Republic of Germany. Coke production amounted to 4,436,000 tons, crude iron to 3,103,000 tons, crude steel to 3,460,000 tons (1959). The average depth of the shafts is 1,800 feet; the average thickness of the coal seams five feet.

28 The ODENWALD, the north-easterly of the ridges which follow the course of the Upper Rhine, has the same geological structure as the rest—a crystalline rock base with a coloured sandstone covering. In the Odenwald and its neighbourhood there are numerous traces of Carolingian culture (Lorsch, Seligenstadt). View of the health resort of REICHELSHEIM.

29 The old imperial city of SPEYER on the left bank of the Rhine has been a cathedral town since the 7th century. It was the favourite residence of the Salic emperors and the scene of numerous imperial Diets. The cathedral was founded in 1030 by Conrad II and vaulted at the end of the 11th century under Henry IV. Eight German emperors and kings lie buried in its crypt. The plate shows the tomb of King Rudolf of Habsburg.

30 WORMS was already inhabited by the Celts and later by the Romans. At the time of the Migration of Peoples in the 5th century it was the capital of the Burgundians, mentioned in the *Nibelungenlied*. Almost a hundred Diets were held in the town (in 1521 the Diet before which Luther appeared). In the town, which has often suffered heavy destruction (most recently in the Second World War) the cathedral has been preserved untouched. It is built of red sandstone (1171–1240) like all large buildings on the Upper Rhine. The picture shows the west chancel which was finished last.

31 MICHELSTADT: view of the town hall built in 1484. In the background the tower of the town church.

32 Landscape of LOWER FRANCONIA.

33 The pilgrims' Church of the VIERZEHNHEILIGEN in Central Franconia, situated on a height overlooking the Main, is dedicated to the 14 *Nothelfer*, or helpers in need. The new building of 1743–72, which was designed by Balthasar Neumann, is among the most spectacular achievements in spatial effect of German Baroque. View of the high altar with the pilgrims' altar in the foreground.

34 WÜRZBURG, the chief town of Franconia, a bishop's see from 741, owes its wealth of ecclesiastical and secular buildings to the artistic taste of a long line of duke-bishops. Their residence was built (1720–44) by Balthasar Neumann under Bishop Johann Philipp Franz von Schönborn. The staircase-hall is one of the masterpieces of the great architect. It has survived the destruction of the residence, together with the painted ceilings by G. B. Tiepolo.

35–6 The vineyards near WÜRZBURG, where the white *Steinwein*, famous for its delicate earthy taste, grows, were planted partly by the diocese and partly by the monasteries.

35 View of the vineyards.

36 The old Baroque wine vaults of the JULIUS SPITAL in Würzburg, a building of Bishop Julius Echter von Mespelsbrunn (1576–80).

37 MILTENBERG, situated at a bend in the Main between the Spessart and the Odenwald, was once an important trading town in the electorate of Mainz. The market-place with its beamed 15th-century houses and fountain dating from 1583 is the heart of the quaint little town.

38 The town of BAMBERG, built on seven hills in the valley of the Regnitz in Upper Franconia, has been a cathedral town since 1007. For centuries the influence of the Church determined its appearance which has remained unaltered to this very day. The Cathedral of SS. Peter and George, which was planned at the beginning of the 11th century under Emperor Henry II and rebuilt in the 13th century, is in its wealth of sculptural masterpieces next to Naumburg the most precious monument of German medieval art. View of the east chancel and the sub-structure of the east towers with the Portal of Adam (left, beginning of the 13th century).

39 WIESBADEN. Like most of the South German resorts with thermal springs, this town was also a Roman settlement, situated hard by the old Roman boundary, the *limes*. Residence of the Nassau-Usingen family from 1744, capital of the Duchy of Nassau from 1816. The picture shows the pump-room, rebuilt 1904-5, using parts of the old structure of 1810.

40 The main street in the small town of HASSFURT in Lower Franconia, with the town hall dating from 1514 and one of the 16th-century town gates.

1-3 ROTHENBURG on the Tauber is the rare example of a late medieval city that has been preserved in its entirety. Its importance as a Free Imperial city reaches far back into the Middle Ages.

41 The TOWN FORTIFICATIONS date back to the 14th and 15th centuries, the outer gateway, just visible in the picture, to the 17th.

42 The old double-arched BRIDGE across the Tauber was built in 1330.

43 By using the earlier Gothic structure whose tower-crowned portion just appears to the left of the picture, the TOWN HALL was developed by J. Wolff of Nuremberg, beginning in 1572, into one of the most impressive monuments of the *bourgeoisie*. The balcony to the front dates from 1681.

44 MAINZ lies, like all the important Roman founda-tions on the Rhine, on the left bank of the river. In early Christian times it was already the seat of a bishopric, and in the Middle Ages, as one of the three ecclesiastical electoral principalities, the most powerful archbishopric next to Trier and Cologne. The town was leader of the Rhenish League of Cities founded in 1254. Here it was that Gutenberg in-vented printing (mid-15th century) and Matthias Grünewald was active at the Mainz Court of Arch-bishop Albrecht (beginning of the 16th century). As a fortress and garrison town Mainz was often de-stroyed. It was damaged particularly severely during the Second World War. The Cathedral of St Martin which survived the destruction was begun at the end of the 10th century and received its present shape in

the 12th and 13th centuries. Our picture shows the view of the central tower with transept and west apse, a self-contained group of magnificent Late Hohenstaufen architecture. The ornamental domes of the towers date from the 18th century.

45-6 FRANKFURT-AM-MAIN (population 643,000), one of the most important commercial and financial centres of Germany, is mentioned as early as 793 as royal palace and in 876 as capital of the Kingdom of the East Franks. From the time of the Hohenstaufens the German kings were elected here and from 1562 the emperors crowned. In 1764 the young Goethe witnessed here the coronation of Joseph II.

45 The 'ROMER' (old town hall), showing its central portion which dates from 1405. This contains the Emperor's Hall, from whose balcony the newly chosen Holy Roman Emperor showed himself to the people below.

46 The newly restored RIVER FRONT with the CATHEDRAL in the background. From 1356 the cathedral was the legally appointed place for the election of the German kings. It dates from the 13th and 14th centuries, the tower in the lower portion from the beginning of the 15th, the spire only from 1877.

47-8 MANNHEIM developed in the 17th century from a citadel into a town in which the electors of the Palatinate had, from 1720 onwards, their official residence. Since the 19th century Mannheim has grown into an important industrial and commercial centre whose favourable situation on the Rhine and Neckar led to the development of a great inland port.

48 The STATE THEATRE (Nationaltheater) comprises a large and a small hall and is a representative example of post-war German theatre-architecture. The architect was Gerhard Weber; it was completed in 1957.

49-56 The RHINE. About 700 miles long, it is navigable from Rheinfelden to the mouth and forms the frontier between France and Germany in the southern portion of its canalized section, the Upper Rhine. The Middle Rhine between Bingen and Bonn has dug for itself a deep valley with many meanderings through the Rhenish slate mountains. More than thirty castles (most of them destroyed in 1689) and many once-important places are mirrored in its waters which join up in a defile with one of the most important of Central European trade routes.

49 The MARKSBURG, standing above Braubach on the right bank of the Rhine, came into the possession of the counts of Katzenelnbogen in 1283. The outworks date from the 17th and 18th centuries. The whole structure was restored about 1900 but severely damaged in 1945. It has now again been restored.

50 The PFALZGRAFENSTEIN stands on a rock which rises out of the river in front of the small town of Caub. The castle was originally built in 1326 by King Ludwig the Bavarian to safeguard the levying of the Rhine tolls. It later belonged to the counts palatine of the Rhine. The fortifications as well as the arched tower date from the 17th century. This small fortress was used by Blücher to guard his army's crossing of the Rhine (New Year 1813–14). This was the last 'modern' function fulfilled by any of the Rhineland castles.

51 The echo of the LORELEI or Lurlei rock that juts steeply into the Rhine inspired Clemens Brentano's Lore-Lay-Poem (1800). This is the first time that the legend of the dangerous mermaid who ensnares passing sailors with her song makes its appearance. In Heine's folk-song version set to music by Silcher it later became widely popular. View upstream from the left bank of the Rhine.

52 The pilgrims' church of BORNHOFFEN on the right bank of the Rhine is said to have been founded by the sister of the 'hostile brothers', each of whom had his castle on the slope above it. A huge fortified wall and a deep moat separate the two castles of Sterrenberg (mentioned in the 12th century as imperial castle and feudal tenure of the Herren von Bolanden) and Liebestein (in the possession of the counts of Sponheim during the 14th century).

53 OBERWESEL, on the left bank of the Rhine, with its medieval fortifications. Above the town the parish Church of St Martin; in the foreground the lively traffic of tugs of many nationalities.

54–5 BACHARACH on the left bank of the Rhine was a prosperous town in the Middle Ages as a trading centre for Rhineland wines. View of a tower belonging to the town fortifications, which also enclose part of the vineyards.

56 ST GOARSHAUSEN on the right bank of the Rhine is overhung by the Castle of Katzenelnbogen. In 1806 the castle was razed to the ground. It was later rebuilt.

57 The wine-growing centre of COCHEM on the Mosel ceased to be part of the Empire in 1294 and passed into the possession of the archbishopric of Trier. In 1332 it was granted town status. The castle, founded in 1207, was destroyed by the French in 1689 but rebuilt 1869–78.

58–9 TRIER (*Augusta Treverorum*) was founded in 15 B.C. by Augustus on the site of an old sanctuary of the Celtic-Germanic Treveri. From 285 to 400 it was the residence of the Roman emperors for the western part of the Empire. The town belonged to the Franks from 460. In the 10th century it joined the German Reich. As seat of the archbishop and later electors Trier was an important town throughout the whole of the Middle Ages. It was severely damaged in the last war.

58 View from the west of the CATHEDRAL and the CHURCH OF OUR LADY, both built on Roman foundations. The cathedral and the Church of Our Lady received their present shape in the 11th and 13th centuries respectively.

59 The PORTA NIGRA (4th century) is the northern gate of the former Roman wall round the town, about four miles long. To the left can be seen the apse of the Church of St Simeon which in the 12th century was built into the structure of the gate.

60 ELTZ CASTLE, situated on a small tributary of the same name to the left of the Moselle in the Eifel region, was the seat of the counts of Eltz. Despite the fact that it was restored in 1920 after having been burned down, it is still an unusual embodiment of the Romantic image of the medieval German castle.

61 LIMBURG on the lower course of the Lahn became a town at the beginning of the 13th century and was the seat of a bishopric from 1827. The town is dominated by the powerful collegiate Church of St George, the 'cathedral', which was founded in 909 by the Salic ruler Konrad Kurzbold and erected in its present shape in 1213–42. It is a typical monument of Rhenish-Hohenstaufen architecture.

62 MARBURG on the Lahn. View from the south-east of the old town, crowned by the castle, the residence of the counts of Hesse from 1247 onwards. It was here that Count Philipp, who founded the University of Marburg, brought together the two religious reformers, Zwinghi and Luther for their discussion of 1529.

63 The little town of FRITZLAR which grew out of a Benedictine abbey founded by Boniface in 740, was at its most prosperous in the centuries of the Saxon and Early Hohenstaufen emperors. From 940 approximately, Fritzlar was a royal palace and here Imperial Diets met in 953 and 954. The MARKET-PLACE with the merchants' house of 1840 and the market fountain of 1564.

64 WETZLAR on the Lahn. View of the town and the collegiate Church of St Mary from the ruined castle of Kalsmunt. In the foreground, the Leitz works. Together with other industrial enterprises such as iron foundries and steel works, these have transformed the sleepy little imperial town of former days into a busy industrial centre. From 1693 until 1806 it was the seat of the Imperial Supreme Court, to which the young Goethe was attached as a law student in 1772.

65 HOMBERG on the Efze. First mentioned in 1162, it has beautiful half-timbered houses typical of Hesse.

66 ALSFELD in Upper Hesse was founded in 1222 by the Landgrave of Thuringia along the important highway linking Hesse and Thuringia, and developed rapidly during the 13th century. Its town hall of 1512, with its open, stone ground floor and beamed superstructure whose façade is crowned by two slate-covered small towers, stands out as one of the loveliest of its kind (Plate 31).

67 The SIEBENGEBIRGE opposite Bonn. View of the DRACHENFELS.

68 AUTOBAHN (linking Frankfurt-am-Main with Cologne) in the western part of the Westerwald, a wooded section of Rhineland slate mountains with volcanic peaks.

69 BONN—Castra Bonnensia in Roman times—has been the seat of the West German Federal Government since 1949. As the residence of the archbishop-electors of Cologne (1273–1794) it became a centre of German culture. Under the Elector Max Friedrich an academy was founded in 1777 from which the famous university developed. In 1770 Ludwig van Beethoven was born in Bonn. Our plate shows the east chancel and the central tower of the minster, a work of 12th-century Rhenish architecture.

70 The hot springs of AACHEN (aquae) made it into a spa as early as Roman times. Charlemagne built himself a palace on the hill where the springs emerge. The Chapel Palatine, a centralized structure built from a Byzantine model, has been preserved as the nucleus of the minster. It used to be the coronation church of the German emperors and contains, apart from Charlemagne's stately throne, undoubtedly the richest assembly of ecclesiastical treasures that have been preserved. View of the western part of the upper gallery with the imperial throne.

71-3 COLOGNE (population 750,000), the large industrial town and trading centre on the Rhine, was founded in 38 B.C. by the Roman general, Agrippa. From the 10th century onwards the archbishops of Cologne played a prominent part in the affairs of the Empire as rulers and later as electors. The town became one of the most active members of the Hanseatic League and was always a centre of Christian culture.

71 Of the many and important churches of the town none remained undamaged. A small CHAPEL was built in the ruins of St Columba's by Gottfried Böhm in 1949; the statue of St Mary on the chancel wall was rescued undamaged from the rubble. The sculptures on the left are by Ewald Mataré, and the windows by Gies.

72 Among the venerable churches of 'holy Cologne' the CATHEDRAL stands out, the most impressive monument of German High Gothic style along the Rhine. The building begun in 1248, was left unfinished for a long time and was not completed until the 19th century, to which a large part of the main aisle and both spires belong.

73 The RHINE BRIDGE at Cologne-Mülheim, built 1127–9, and after its destruction rebuilt 1951. Example of a suspension bridge with long span (approx. 344 yards).

74 DÜSSELDORF (population 680,000), the residence of the rulers of Berg from 1348 onwards and later part of the Palatinate is today capital of the province of North-Rhine Westphalia. As the centre of Rhineland and Westphalian industry it contains important industrial installations (Mannesmann, DKW, Schlömann). The Art Academy, built in the 18th century, enjoys a good reputation. In the absence of really 'great' history there arose here one of the busiest and most elegant metropolitan centres of Germany. Our plate shows the Wilhelm-Marx skyscraper in the centre of the town built by Wilhelm Kreis 1922–4.

75–79, 81 The INDUSTRIAL AREA along the River Ruhr grew up as a result of the rich resources of coal there. Workable seams of an average thickness of 3 feet 6 inches are found down to a depth of nearly 4,000 feet. It is calculated that they will yield 34.2 milliard tons. Coal production in 1959 amounted to 125,600,000 tons.

75 SIEGEN in Westphalia. The rolling mills at Gontermann & Peiper. The reserves of iron ore in the Sieg country are estimated at about 27 million tons.

76 ESSEN. The Bonifacius pit. Workers at the coal face 2,600 feet below ground. Essen, which is the chief town of the Ruhr district, has twenty-two pits within the town boundary alone, and in addition to this it has the Krupp works and many other great industries. The appearance of the town has been so dominated by industry since the 19th century that the Ottonian collegiate church has been completely pushed into the background. This church is, however, evidence of the cultural age of the Ruhr valley.

77 Coal barges on the RHINE-HERNE CANAL, a section of the canal running from Duisburg to Hamburg.

78 View of the DUISBURG copper foundry, and the Demag works. Duisburg is a major industrial centre, but it is particularly important as a river port, situated as it is at the confluence of the rivers Ruhr and Rhine. 22,119,000 tons of goods moved through the docks at Duisburg in 1954.

79 The GERMANIA MINE near Dortmund with one of the new townships which have sprung up since the war.

80 SOEST in Westphalia. View of the chancel, transept, and the mighty west tower of the collegiate Church of St Patroclus. Soest was one of the most important Hansa towns of the interior. (It had charge of the keys to the treasury chest of Novgorod.) Its history, that reaches back to Merovingian times, is full, in the Middle Ages, of constant struggles with the Archbishop of Cologne. One expression of this conflict is the collegiate church of which the eastern portions belong to Cologne foundation, but the western parts to the town. It has created for itself in the tower a symbol of power and freedom (13th century).

81 DORTMUND. View of the 'Westfalen' foundry, one of the works of the Hoesch Company, with agricultural land in the foreground. Such a scene is typical of the Ruhr district. The land lying between the factories and mines is very fertile and is intensively cultivated.

82 XANTEN on the Lower Rhine. Towers and cloisters of the collegiate Church of St Victor, which was begun in the 13th century. The town has grown up on Roman foundations. Varus marched with his legions against the Germans out of *Castra Vetera*, founded 15 B.C. St Victor, leader of the Theban Legion is said to have died a martyr's death here.

83 CORVEY on the River Weser. View of the west wall of the monastery church, which belongs to one of the oldest Benedictine monasteries in Saxony. It was founded at the beginning of the 9th century as a

companion monastery to the great abbey at Corbie in Picardy, in an area which had just been conquered by Charlemagne. The western parts of this magnificent building are some of the few remaining examples of the art of building in Carolingian times. (The upper parts of the tower and intermediate storey date from the 12th century.)

84 MÜNSTER, an old Hanseatic town, is the intellectual centre of Westphalia. The magnificent palaces (mostly 18th century) of the nobility and high clergy, gave the town a character all its own. The reconstructed episcopal palace is today the seat of the university. The Gothic interior of the Lamberti Church, built about 1450.

85 OSNABRÜCK has been an episcopal see since Carolingian times. View of parts of the town fortifications and old town.

86 The moated castle of GEMEN near Borken in Westphalia. The place is a very ancient strongpoint of the Chamaves (hence the name of Gemen) against the Brukteri. Until 1802 Gemen came directly under the jurisdiction of the Empire. The building of 1411, to which additions were made during the 17th century, stands on the massive foundation walls of an earlier building.

87 VISCHERING CASTLE, north-west of Lüdinghausen, owned by the counts of Droste-Vischering since early times and, like Gemen Castle, a typical Westphalian noble's residence. The buildings seen in this picture date from the 16th century.

88–9 EAST FRIESLAND. The plain between the rivers Ems and Weser is used chiefly for pastoral farming. The extensive moors are a source of peat for fuel. Oil is obtained in the southern part between Lingen and the Dutch border.

88 An East Friesian FARM.

89 A moorland SETTLEMENT.

90 LEMGO. View of the town hall and the towers of the Church of St Nicholas. The wonderful gables of the chemist's shop adjoining the town hall can

be seen on the left of the picture. These were built in 1612. This little town situated in the former principality of Lippe was a member of the Hanseatic League and reached the peak of its fortune in the 15th and 16th centuries. It grew rich chiefly through trade with Flanders.

91–2 BREMEN (population 535,000). Since early times a Free Imperial and Hanseatic town. Like Hamburg, it is an independent State and has its own traditional form of administration. It is an important port. In Carolingian times it was a bishop's see, and the records of 967 refer to it as a market town. Archbishop Adalbert of Bremen, the guardian of Emperor Henry IV, planned his northern patriarchate from here in the 11th century. The town's many ancient buildings suffered severe damage during the last war.

91 The BÖTTCHERSTRASSE. This was built between 1924 and 1928 by the Hanseatic merchant Ludwig Roselius (the originator of Kaffee Hag) to old designs. It was largely destroyed during the war, but has been rebuilt and is now a museum and centre of handicrafts and culture in the town.

92 The HARBOUR at night. In 1959 the turnover of goods amounted to 4,146,000 tons to the inland waterways, and 14,000,000 tons for overseas. Part of the shipping traffic goes via Bremerhaven, a port nearer the mouth of the river.

93 WINDMILLS near Greetsiel on the East Friesian coast. A landscape reminiscent of Holland.

94 SHIPS on the River Weser at Vegesack near Bremen.

95 MARSHLANDS near Worpswede. Around 1900 the little town housed the well-known artists' colony whose members included R. M. Rilke, Paula Becker-Modersohn, and the sculptor Hoetger, who helped to create the Böttcherstrasse.

96 KASSEL. The town lies on the left bank of the River Fulda between the Habicht and Kaufunger forests. Once residence of the counts and later of the electors of Hessen, it developed into a city in the 19th century thanks to its favourable position as a communications

link. The Wilhelmshöhe Park, the electors' summer residence near Kassel, is 'perhaps the most grandiose blending of architecture and landscape ever attempted in the Baroque style' (Dehio). The designs for the park were made by the Italian Guernieri in 1701. From the 'Oktogon', which conceals a reservoir, water pours down over the artificial cascade of steps and feeds the fountains. In the background is the town of Kassel.

97 RHÖN. View from the Heidelstein (3,000 feet) towards the Eierhank and the Dammersfeld peak (3,000 feet). This plateau of the Rhön is largely meadowland and moorland. It lies between the Upper Fulda, the Upper Werra, and the River Saale (in Franconia), and is dominated by peaks of volcanic rock rising to 3,150 feet.

98 FULDA. Interior of St Michael's Church. This was built as a cemetery chapel in the form of a rotunda following early Christian example. It was begun in the 9th century and the present building was finished at the end of the 10th century. Fulda was famed for the monastery which was founded here in 744 by a disciple of St Boniface.

99 HILDESHEIM. View of the bay windows of the Templar House and part of the neighbouring Wedekind House, two of the most beautiful buildings which stood in the town market-place before its destruction. From the 9th century onwards Hildesheim was a bishop's see. In the early part of the 10th century the town was one of the most important centres in the Empire at the time of Bishop Bernward. Later, it became independent and joined the Hanseatic League in 1241. Its wonderful masterpieces of civic architecture were almost completely destroyed during the last war. (The Templar House was not damaged, but the Wedekind House has unfortunately been replaced by a modern building.)

100 EINBECK. Achieved the status of town in 1272, and became the residence of the princes of Grubenhagen. Famous for its beer since the 15th century. This is a view of the town hall, which was built in 1550 and is a wonderful example of architecture incorporating timber panelling on the grand scale.

101 The HARZ MOUNTAINS rise like an island from the North German plain, which barely exceeds 300 feet elsewhere. It is a tilted plateau of grey wacke and slate which slopes from the north-west to the south-east and is deeply indented by valleys above which ridges and peaks rise. The highest of these, and thus the highest mountain in North Germany is the Brocken (3,800 feet). It is also called the Blocksberg on account of its weathered blocks of granite. Since the 14th century it has been regarded as the place to which the witches come riding on Walpurgis-night.

102 View of GOSLAR, situated on the northern edge of the Harz Mountains. The town owes its existence to the finding of a vein of silver in the hills in the 10th century. It became the favourite resort of the Saxon and Salic emperors, and the Romanesque style of the imperial palace is a reminder of them. The masterpieces of civic architecture have remained intact.

103 QUEDLINBURG. View of the collegiate church from the south-east with the castle in the background. Henry I built this castle in 924 as a fortification against the incursions of the Hungarians. The keep (Fliehburg) became the residence of his wife Mathilda during her widowhood and she founded a convent here. The castle stands next to the Romanesque church high above the fertile plain.

104 WOLFSBURG, a town of Lower Saxony north-west of Brunswick, is now the chief centre for the motor industry which has developed from the Volkswagen Works, first established in an area containing four villages.

105-6 HANOVER is an important industrial and trading centre. It was founded about 1200 and has changed rulers many times. From 1636 it was the residence of the Kalenberg-Celle line of the House of Guelph. In 1714 when the dukes inherited the English throne, Hanover became united with England through the person of the king, and remained so until 1837. During the last war the town suffered great loss through the destruction of many of its famous buildings, as, for example, the Leibnitz House dating from the 17th century.

105 HERRENHAUSEN PALACE with the gardens, which are modelled on those of Versailles.

106 The tower of the rebuilt market church (Marktkirche) seen from the Ballhof. Originally built about 1350, it is a beautiful example of Lower Saxon brick architecture.

107 Heathland FARMS near Celle.

108-9 BRUNSWICK (Braunschweig). The town was founded by the Guelph duke Henry, whose famous Lion monument still stands in the square by the cathedral. The town developed into an important centre of trade for the German interior in the 13th century, and became an outpost of the Hanseatic League in Lower Saxony. From 1753 onwards Brunswick was the residence of the dukes of Braunschweig-Wolfenbüttel. Its many churches and wealth of civic architecture are evidence of its long history. Irreplaceable damage was done to the town during the last war.

108 The new building of the TECHNICAL HIGH SCHOOL. In the left background can be seen the cathedral towers, and on the right are the unsymmetrical towers of St Andrew's.

109 View of the gables at the eastern end of the CLOTHWORKERS' HALL, which was built in 1591 by Balthasar Kircher. In the background is the chancel of St Martin's Church (Martinikirche).

110 The New Town Gate at TANGERMÜNDE, built in 1420. Until the end of the 15th century the town was the chief seat of the margrave of Brandenburg. Emperor Charles IV lived here from time to time between 1373 and 1377; he fortified the town, which is an important place for river traffic on the Elbe. The magnificent brickwork architecture of the fortifications is typical of the towns of the Altmark (cf. Salzwedel, Plate 112) and of North-east Germany.

111 Looking across the RIVER ELBE towards Tangermünde. The lower reaches of the river are connected by an intricate system of canals with the River Oder, as a result of which large parts of Brandenburg and Mecklenburg can be reached by inland waterways.

112 The earliest records of SALZWEDEL in the Altmark are dated 1112; it achieved town status in 1233. Evidence of its importance as a city—it was a member of the Hanseatic League from 1263—can be seen from this picture of the strong town gates and bastions, which were built to withstand artillery fire.

113 MAGDEBURG. The Wise Virgins. Part of the decoration of the cathedral doorway. They date from the first half of the 13th century. Historically and in their quality they are akin to the work of the great Bamberg master. Magdeburg was already a centre of border trade at the time of Charlemagne, and following the establishment of the archbishopric there in 968 it became the spiritual centre of the eastern part of Germany. The cathedral, which was begun by Otto I, was rebuilt at the beginning of the 13th century.

114-15 LÜNEBURG, situated on the River Ilmenau, a tributary of the Elbe, was once an influential member of the Hanseatic League. It reached the peak of its fortunes rather too early as a result of rich deposits of salt.

114 Side view of the market front of the TOWN HALL, which was built in 1720. The figures in the niches are from an earlier, 16th-century, wall.

115 These HOUSES date from its heyday between the 14th and 16th centuries. The step-gables usually have a pulley hoist jutting out from the top.

116 Heath LANDSCAPE. Its great pictorial beauty belies its economic importance. Sheep farming and beekeeping are carried on here, and oil is found north of Celle.

117-19 HAMBURG (population 1,800,000), free State and Hanseatic town. It is the terminus of a huge system of inland waterways, above all, those of the River Elbe. It is also Germany's biggest port. Here, at the crossing of the Alster, Charlemagne placed a bastion against the Slavonic tribes. Trading began early. In 1241 the citizens made a protective agreement with Lübeck, extending it to Bremen in 1259, and this agreement became the basis of the German Hanseatic League. The later development of trade with America resulted in an enormous growth of the town. One third of the old town was destroyed by fire in 1842, and during the last war the city was bombed almost to ruins. Rebuilding on modern lines has since been carried out.

117 Aerial view of the town and docks.

118 View across the HARBOUR to St Michael's Church (Michaelskirche)—the 'Michel' which is the symbol of the town. The turnover of trade in 1959 was 29,040,000 tons for overseas, and 6,704,000 tons by way of the inland waterways.

119 Newly built blocks of FLATS at the Grindel.

120 Slightly away from the River Elbe, on the left bank below Hamburg is STADE, the former capital of the pricipality of Bremen. View of the old harbour.

121 The NORTH SEA. Scene from Wyk on the island of Föhr.

122 The 'ALTES LAND'. This is the name given to a densely populated area of river marshland which lies on the left of the River Elbe between Hamburg and Stade. Descendants of the Flemish settlers still live in these neat houses, which are examples of Lower Saxon timber-framed buildings.

123 HALLIG HOOGE. The Halligs are small islands among the mudflats and muddy shallows along the west coast of Schleswig-Holstein. They are the remains of mainland marshes which have been swamped by the high tides. The houses here are built on artificial mounds about 12 to 15 feet high called 'Warften', and the surrounding pasture-land is at the mercy of the high tides and storms.

124 KOOGE, North Friesland. This is an area which has been reclaimed from the North Sea, and is drained and protected by canals and dikes.

125 SCHOBÜLL CHURCH, north-west of Husum. In the background are the mudflats and the Hallig coast. It is a typical country church of Schleswig-Holstein: built of brick, with a single nave and a flat-walled chancel (13th century).

126 FLENSBURG. View from the harbour towards the town and the castle. Along the east coast of Schleswig-Holstein are long, fiord-like indentations where the sea penetrates far inland, and this fact permits the establishment of large ports in protected positions—in complete contrast to the west coast.

127 AHRENSBURG CASTLE, a manor in Schleswig-Holstein, built about 1594.

128-9 LÜBECK was founded in 1143 by settlers from Westphalia, and became a free town in 1226. Its extensive trade, especially with the north and east, led to the establishment of the Hanseatic League. The town was badly damaged in 1942.

128 The HOLSTEIN GATE, a brick structure completed in 1477.

129 The HOSPITAL OF THE HOLY GHOST (Heilig-Geist-Spital). The best remaining example of a medieval communal institution. It was founded in the middle of the 13th century and fulfils its purpose today as a home for the aged.

130 WISMAR. This town represented the Wend district in the federation of towns which became the Hanseatic League. Its churches are some of the greatest monuments of North German Gothic architecture in brick. On the left of the picture is the Church of St George (14th and 15th centuries) and on the right the tower of St Mary's (15th century).

131 The cathedral at HAVELBERG came into being in the early period of the conversion of the Wends to Christianity. It was founded in 946. This picture shows the impressive western structure which was built towards the end of the 13th century.

132 Birch trees and sand. A typical scene in BRANDENBURG and the Havel country.

133 Pine trees on the shores of LAKE MÜGGEL, east of Berlin.

134 BRICKWORKS at GLINDOW near Werder with their old-fashioned, beautiful chimneys. Both to the north and south of Berlin there are many brickworks

along the River Havel, which from time immemorial have supplied the material for the austere buildings of the Brandenburg district.

-141 BERLIN. The city's development mirrors the rise of the Hohenzollerns from electors of Brandenburg to kings of Prussia and finally emperors of Germany. Berlin did not become a major capital city until the second half of the 19th century; in 1945 it had almost 4½ million inhabitants. The town was badly damaged during the last war, and it has been hard hit by the post-war division into sectors and its isolated situation in the Eastern Zone of Germany.

135 The equestrian statue of the GREAT ELECTOR has also been preserved intact, and this picture shows it at its new site in front of Charlottenburg Castle. Originally it stood behind Berlin Castle. Charlottenburg, the central building of which can be seen in the background, was built in 1695 as the summer residence of Electress Sophie-Charlotte, and was later added to by the architect Eosander von Goethe.

136 The BRANDENBURG GATE. A triumphal arch forming a gateway to the city at the beginning of the 'Linden'. It was built in 1788–91 by K. G. Langhans, who based it on the Propylaeum, and it was crowned by a bronze quadriga by the sculptor Schadow. Today it forms the sector boundary.

137 The STALIN ALLEE, the main ceremonial way and showpiece of the Eastern Sector of Berlin, in Soviet-style architecture of the Stalin era.

138 The CONGRESS HALL was the American contribution to the International Building Exhibition in Berlin in 1957. The architect was Hugh A. Stubbins, working with the Berlin architects W. Duttmann and F. Mocken.

139 The HANSA QUARTER alongside the Zoological Garden was founded on the occasion of the International Building Exhibition in 1957. The steel wire sculpture is by Hans Ullmann. The Roman Catholic Church of St Asgar in the background was designed by Willy Kreuer.

140 The CONCERT HALL of the Academy of Music in Charlottenburg.

141 The historical CENTRE OF BERLIN owed its appearance mainly to the buildings of the Baroque period. Berlin Castle, which was one of the major works of the architect and sculptor Andreas Schlüter (1664–1714), was blown up and removed after the war. The series of heads of dying warriors in the courtyard of the armoury have remained as the epitome of true Baroque sculpture.

142 TEGEL CASTLE near Berlin. Originally a hunting-lodge of the Great Elector, it was bought by the Humboldt family and remodelled by Karl Friedrich Schinkel. Wilhelm von Humboldt lived here, and in the park is the burying-place of the family with the graves of Alexander (1769–1859) and Wilhelm (1767–1835). On the top of the column is a copy of a statue by Thorwaldsen.

143–4 The residential town of POTSDAM on the River Havel near Berlin is above all a creation of Frederick William I, the 'Soldier King', and was the favourite residence of the Prussian kings. Frederick William I had a town built in Dutch style around the old Wendish fishing village and the elector's hunting lodge. His son, Frederick II (the Great), added to it and made it more beautiful with his palaces.

143 SANSSOUCI was built in 1745–7 to a design by the king, who also had the great park laid out at the foot of his summer residence.

144 POTSDAM. The tea pavilion in the park at Sanssouci.

145 JÜTERBOG in Brandenburg. A town site since 1174, it belonged until 1635 to the archbishopric of Magdeburg. Of its medieval town walls three gates still remain. On each hangs a club with the inscription:

'He who gives his children bread
And later is himself in need,
Shall with this club be battered till he's dead.'

146 ZINNA MONASTERY not far from Jüterbog. These 15th-century buildings belong to an Order of the Cistercians which was founded in 1170.

147 STENDAL in the Altmark was founded in 1160 by Albert the Bear. The township became a respected member of the Hanseatic League, and in the 15th century it was the chief town in an alliance of towns of the Altmark. The statue of Roland, dating from 1525, stands in front of the town hall, and in the background the towers of St Mary's, dating from the 15th century, can be seen.

148 The statue of Roland at the town hall in BRANDEN-BURG on the River Havel (18½ feet high and erected in 1474) opposite the Storbeck House dating from 1543. On the right is the tower of St Catherine's Church. The Wendish *Brennabor* was conquered by King Henry I from the Slavonic tribes of the Havel country, and Otto the Great founded a bishopric on the cathedral island, which was to convert the east to Christianity. It was finally fortified by Albert the Bear, the first margrave of Brandenburg. The figure of Roland here is, as it is in many North German towns, the symbol of the town's independence.

149 Fishing boats at NIDDEN on the spit of land lying between the Baltic Sea and the Bay of Courland (Kurisches Haff).

150 KÖNIGSBERG. View of the 'Kneiphof', an island around which the River Pregel flows and on which are situated the cathedral and the old university buildings. The town grew up in the 13th century out of a festival of the Teutonic Order. The Grand Master of the Order lived here from 1457, and later, after 1525, the Duke of Prussia resided here in his capacity of Polish feudal lord. When the duchy became part of Brandenburg, Königsberg remained the second capital and seat. In 1701 it was the scene of the coronation of the first king 'in Prussia'. Following the defeat of 1806, the resurgence of Prussia under the guidance of such men as Stein and Scharnhorst was directed from the Royal Court then in residence at Königsberg. The university was founded in 1544, and Immanuel Kant was professor there from 1770 to 1794.

151 The MARIENBURG on the River Nogat was founded in 1280 as residence of a commander of the Teutonic Order. The Grand Master moved his seat of residence here from Venice in 1309. It was then that the Great Refectory was built—a masterpiece of Gothic architecture. Between 1380 and 1389 the crowning group of the summer and winter refectories was added. After the defeat of the Order at Tannen-berg in 1410 the Marienburg became Polish until 1772. At the end of the 18th century the great Prussian architect Friedrich Gilly drew attention to the ruined buildings and as a result they were later restored. The Marienburg was completely destroyed during the last war.

152 HEILSBERG CASTLE was founded in 1241 as a castle of the Teutonic Order, but was then given to the bishop of Ermland, and the bishops continued to live there until the 18th century. The huge quad-rangle with its tiled roofing and two-storied cloisters which rest on granite columns, was built in the second half of the 14th century.

153 The CATHEDRAL OF ST MARY (Mariendom) at Kolberg. Built in the 13th century, its great west front reveals the spirit and energy of the new settlers. This Pomeranian town grew up out of a Slavonic festival. It became the seat of a prebendary in 1065, and joined the Hanseatic League in 1284.

154 DANZIG on the River Mottlau near the mouth of the Vistula. It was once the chief town of the duchy of Pommerellen, but became the property of the Teu-tonic Order in 1306. In 1316 it joined the Hanseatic League and became the leading town of the area of East German colonization, and, in fact, one of the most important trading centres of the Middle Ages. From 1454 to 1772 it was a Polish protectorate, then became part of Prussia. From 1919 to 1939 it was a free State under the auspices of the League of Nations, and since 1945 it has been Polish again. The great west tower of St Mary's (Marienkirche) rises above the 16th- and 17th-century houses, which show the extensive influence of Dutch building styles. The town was almost completely destroyed during the last war. The Church of St Mary has since been rebuilt.

155 KÜSTRIN CASTLE on the River Oder was the residence of a branch of the family of the electors of Brandenburg in the 16th century. It was built by the margrave John. Crown Prince Frederick was

detained in Küstrin in 1730; after being pardoned he remained there to study the fundamentals of State administration.

156 The 'ODERBRUCH', low-lying fertile country along the west bank of the River Oder, was originally a swampy wilderness, and was drained between 1746 and 1753 at the time of Frederick the Great. Villages with their half-timbered houses grew up to house the colonists who were brought in by the king from the Palatinate, Swabia, and Poland.

157 Houses in the ERZGEBIRGE (Ore Mountains) near ZINNWALD on the Czechoslovak border. The climate of this mountainous border country between Saxony and Bohemia is cold, and the soil is poor, so that meadows and agricultural land give place to extensive pine forests. Despite this, the district is densely populated because it possesses rich deposits of minerals such as silver, cobalt, nickel, bismuth, and copper; more recently, uranium has been found there. The local domestic industries produce embroidery, textile fabrics, glassware, and toys.

158 Below Cottbus the RIVER SPREE divides into a network of branches known as the SPREEWALD (Spree forest), in which remnants of Wendish culture with its own language and customs can still be found today. The individual farms use boats to communicate with each other.

159 The CHURCH OF ST MAURICE at Mittenwalde. Paul Gerhardt, one of the greatest writers of hymns in the Protestant Church, was minister here from 1651 to 1657.

160 FRANKFURT-AN-DER-ODER grew up at an important river crossing point between Germany and Poland, and achieved the status of a town in 1253. The front of the 15th-century town hall shows the high degree of ornamentation developed in the long tradition of border-country brick architecture.

161 BAUTZEN, chief town of western Upper Lusatia (Oberlausitz), lies on the upper course of the River Spree. The town flourished in the 13th century thanks to its position on the old east to west trade route, the 'Hohe Landstrasse'. The Ortenburg, a castle which was built between 1483 and 1486, towers above the town. Recently, on orders from the State, Bautzen has been made the centre of a Wendish culture movement with an official second language.

162 The River Oder near MALTSCH, an industrial centre (sugar, cellulose, paper) and shipping point for the Waldenburg coal-mine.

163-4 GÖRLITZ on the River Neisse. Today it is a frontier town facing the eastern areas now under Polish administration. It has a wealth of houses from the time when Jacob Böhme was cobbler there.

163 The CHURCH OF ST PETER (Peterskirche) seen from the tower of the town hall. The church was built in the 15th century and the towers were added in the 19th century.

164 View of the LOWER MARKET with the beautiful house-fronts dating from the 16th and 17th centuries. In the background is the weighing machine which was put up in 1606. The buildings shown in this picture have remained undamaged.

165 The TOWN HALL, BRESLAU. Details of the east frontage with the bay window built in 1420 and the clock, which dates from 1580. The highly ornamented windows belong to the Princes Hall of the old town hall chapel. This is an example of the asymmetric, picturesque composition of Late Gothic secular architecture. The buildings of the town hall are some of the most important works of this kind. Breslau (Polish: Wroclaw) is the capital town of Silesia, and in the Middle Ages was the seat of an independent principality. In 1335 it was incoporated into Bohemia, in 1527 it became Austrian, and finally, as a result of the wars of Frederick the Great, it became Prussian. In 1945—totally destroyed—it came under Polish administration.

166-8 Glass-blowing and weaving are the most important occupations in the mountains of SILESIA. Gerhart Hauptmann, in his dramas, brought the speech and the hardships endured by these people into the world's literature.

166 The living-room of a SILESIAN HOUSE, with the loom in the corner.

167 The 'Josephinenhütte' GLASSWORKS at Schreiberhau in the Riesengebirge. They were built in 1842.

168 SCHÖMBERG in Silesia with its peculiar porched houses.

169 The wooden church at PONISCHOWITZ in Upper Silesia, with its separate bell-tower. It is said to have been built in 1404, in which case it would be the oldest wooden church in these parts.

170 LEIPZIG. Interior of the Church of St Thomas (Thomaskirche), which was built in the form of a Hall church between 1484 and 1496. Johann Sebastian Bach was organist here from 1723 until his death in 1750. St Thomas's School, and the university which had been founded in 1409, as well as the important trade fairs which were held there, combined in those days to make Leipzig one of the chief centres of culture. Since the 19th century the town has concentrated on the book trade and has achieved fame throughout Europe for this.

171-2 DRESDEN, one-time capital of the Kingdom of Saxony. It was the residence of the Wettins and was of great economic and cultural importance. In Dresden 17th- and 18th-century architecture reached a degree of perfection, particularly at the time of August the Strong, found—north of the Alps—only in Vienna and Salzburg. Thus with the destruction of the city in 1945 many masterpieces such as the Protestant 'Frauenkirche' were lost.

171 The Royal Gate (Kronentor) of the ZWINGER PALACE, after rebuilding. This was originally built between 1711 and 1722 by Matth. Daniel Pöppelmann and was ornamented by the Salzburg sculptor Permoser.

172 The Roman Catholic 'HOFKIRCHE' (Court Church), after rebuilding. It was built between 1738 and 1751 by Gaetano Chiaveri, and is a masterpiece of Italian architecture on German soil. On the left behind the church are the ruins of the palace, and on the right is the Opera House.

173 The HUNTING LODGE, MORITZBURG, of the elector of Saxony was founded in 1542-6 and reconstructed in 1722-30 by Pöppelmann.

174 The SÄCHSISCHE SCHWEIZ ('Saxon Switzerland') mountains through which the River Elbe cuts, and which consist of a plateau of sandstone with a horizontal covering stratum of chalk, both split and cleft in all directions. The fissured and riven nature of the rock has created many adventurous and exciting labyrinths and ravines amongst the columns and rock walls.

175 MEISSEN on the River Elbe. Built in 930 by King Henry I, it was the seat of the margrave of Meissen until 1090. On the rocks above the town rise the cathedral and castle, a group of buildings known as the 'Albrechtsburg', built between 1471 and 1485. The cathedral was begun in 1249 but its west towers are modern. It was here that Johann Friedrich Boettger, during his enforced stay in the castle, discovered the type of china which has made the town world famous.

176 The 'Gothic' house in the park at WÖRLITZ. Franz von Anhalt, whose ideas were influenced by English landscape gardening, had this park laid out in 1764. The architecture of the Romantic period in England also influenced the style of the Gothic house, which was begun in 1772. Here the prince, at the instigation of Lavater, surrounded himself with medieval works of art.

177 SCHMALKALDEN. View of the town church (1437-1506). The place became famous through the meetings of the Protestant princes, who established the Schmalkaldic League here in 1530.

178 ERFURT CATHEDRAL. View from the south-east showing the chancel windows which date from the end of the 14th century, and which have remained intact in all their old glory. This old town, once part of the archbishopric of Mainz, was in the Middle Ages a centre of theology.

179 NAUMBURG. The town grew up in the 11th century around a castle which had been built by the margrave of Meissen and Thuringia, and it became a bishop's

see in 1030. The Cathedral of St Peter and St Paul, which was consecrated in 1242, was built on the foundations of an older building of the 11th century. With two chancels and four towers the new cathedral compares favourably with Bamberg in the wealth of its exterior ornamentation and in the quality of its sculptures. The figures of the founders which adorn the west choir are unique masterpieces, and epitomize the knightly culture of the peak period of the Middle Ages. The picture shows the two founders Ekkehart and Uta.

180 EISLEBEN. The front of the Late Gothic house where Martin Luther died on February 18, 1546. The great reformer was born in this town on November 10, 1483.

181 WITTENBERG. The market-place with the Luther Memorial by Schadow (1821). Behind the memorial is the town hall where Lucas Cranach held office as mayor. Until 1422 this town was the seat of the elector of Saxony and it once possessed a famous university where Martin Luther taught. He inaugurated the Reformation when he pinned his thesis on the door of the castle church in 1517.

182 From 1595 to 1741 the duke of Sachsen-Eisenach resided in EISENACH. Johann Sebastian Bach was born here on March 21, 1695. The Bach family's house now contains a museum of musical instruments, some of which were used by the most famous Bach of all.

183 The WARTBURG. It lies at the north-western tip of the Thuringian Forest near Eisenach, and was built about 1080 by Ludwig the Jumper. It later became the home of the landgraves of Thuringia. The Minnesingers met in the courtyard here at the time of Hermann; St Elizabeth carried out her good works here, and in 1521-2 Luther, while he was living here in hiding from his enemies, completed the translation of the New Testament into German.

184 COBURG CASTLE towers over the town of the same name. The old castle, which was restored after the fire of 1500, was the seat of the counts of Henneberg and the Saxon dukes. Luther stayed here at the time of the Diet of Augsburg and translated the Books of the Prophets and the Psalms. In 1918 Coburg became part of Bavarian Franconia.

185 View of JENA on the Saale, which has taken on a very industrialized appearance owing to the establishment there of the Zeiss works. The university, founded in the 16th century, had its Golden Age under August Duke of Sachsen-Weimar and his minister Goethe, when Fichte, Schelling, Hegel, and Schiller represented the various arts and sciences in the town.

186 View from the Dornburg Castles towards DORNDORF and the fertile Saale valley. Goethe used to retire to the peace and quiet of this part of the country from time to time.

187-9 The name of WEIMAR, the small residential town of the duke of Sachsen-Weimar situated on the River Ilm, became known to the whole world through the works of the great personalities with whom the Duke Karl August surrounded himself. Wieland lived here from 1772 to 1813 as tutor to the princes; Goethe from 1775 to 1832; Herder in his capacity as Superintendent-General from 1776 to 1803: Schiller from 1799 to 1805, and for a while 'Jean Paul', too.

187 The SUMMER HOUSE on the Ilm, a present from the Duke to Goethe, who took up residence there on May 18, 1776. He continued to live here until he moved to the house at the Frauenplan.

188 GOETHE'S HOUSE at the Frauenplan. Given to him as a present by the Duke in 1794. He lived here until his death, receiving important personalities from all parts of Europe. The many collections which Goethe had in his house gave it rather the appearance of a museum—even during his lifetime.

189 Goethe's study.

190 The MEMORIAL OF BUCHENWALD near Weimar, a reminder of one of the most notorious concentration camps of the Hitler era.

191 GÖSSWEINSTEIN, with its castle and pilgrims' church built by Balthasar Neumann. The place towers above the Wiesent valley, which cuts into the plateau of Franconian Switzerland.

192 FORCHHEIM on the River Regnitz in Bavarian Upper Franconia. In the Middle Ages it was the scene of important assemblies of the Imperial States. It possesses beautiful timbered buildings from the 16th and 17th centuries.

193-4 NUREMBERG lies at the crossing of two medieval trade routes, one from Saxony to the Alps and the other from the Rhine to Bohemia and Vienna. Bavarian, Franconian, and Swabian people initiated an aspiring township here, which reached its heyday in the Late Middle Ages and found its greatest expression in the works of the Nuremberg masters, Albrecht Dürer, Veit Stoss, and Peter Vischer. Magnificent churches and splendid architecture remained up to recent times the picture presented by this great centre of trade and craftsmanship, but the last war caused great havoc. Today Nuremberg is an industrial centre.

193 The PRELLER HOUSE, built in 1605 by Jacob Wolff the Elder. It was one of the most splendid civic palaces of the German Renaissance, but has been almost completely destroyed.

194 DÜRER'S HOUSE, built at the beginning of the 15th century.

195 BAYREUTH was the seat of the margraves of Brandenburg-Bayreuth from 1603 to 1769. Its beautiful Rococo buildings were put up at the time of the margrave Frederick, who was married to Wilhelmina, the gifted sister of Frederick the Great. The new palace was built between 1744 and 1773. A memorial fountain with the equestrian figure of the field-marshal margrave Christian Ernst (d. 1712) stands in front of the central building. Alexander von Humboldt made Bayreuth the starting-point of his great life work because of its interesting geological situation, and 'Jean Paul' lived here from 1804 to 1825. From 1876 onwards Richard Wagner made this quiet town the centre of the Bayreuth Festival, which each summer attracts visitors from all parts of the world.

196 ANSBACH developed around a monastery founded by St Gumbertus in the 8th century, and from 1363 it was the seat of the Hohenzollern margrave of Ansbach. The margrave's castle was rebuilt by Gabriel de Gabrielis after the destruction by fire of the old building in 1710.

197 The WILLIBALD CASTLE stands on a height on the right bank of the River Altmühl near Eichstätt. In 745 St Willibald was its first bishop. The imperial fortifications were added in the 14th century at the time of the burgrave of Nuremberg. In 1593 Bishop Konrad von Gemmingen had a new castle erected by the Augsburg master-builder Elias Holl, and this new castle served as residence of the bishops until 1725. It is a rare example of an Early Baroque fortress.

198 ELLINGEN in Franconia belonged to the Teutonic Order from 1216 to 1796 and was the seat of the senior officer of the Franconian Commandery. The Nuremberg Gate dates from the 17th century.

199 The town hall at WOLFRAMSESCHENBACH. Since 1917 the town has been named after its son Wolfram who, born in 1170, was one of the great poets of the peak period of the Middle Ages. The district was a feudal tenure granted by the count of Wertheim to the lords of Eschenbach, whose line became extinct with Wolfram. The Teutonic Order built a commandery here in the 13th century, which was rebuilt in the 17th century and today serves as town hall.

200 DINKELSBÜHL on the River Wörnitz. View of the town with the Late Gothic church of St George in the centre. Dinkelsbühl, like Rothenburg on the Tauber, on the old road from Augsburg to Nuremberg, is regarded as the oldest town in Franconia. It was already a walled town in 928. It remained a country town with corn and cattle market, hardly growing out of its 15th-century fortifications until very recent times. Even today it retains the appearance of an imperial town of the Late Middle Ages.

201-2 NÖRDLINGEN grew into an imperial town at the spot where the basin-like fertile lowlands (Ries) separate the Swabian from the Franconian Jura hills and where the Wörnitz valley forms a link between Middle Franconia and the Swabian Danube valley. The route from Augsburg to Italy forks here to Nuremberg and Würzburg.

201 One of the TOWN GATES dating from the beginning of the 17th century.

202 The steps up to the TOWN HALL, with the tower of St George's in the background.

203 MERKENDORF with its town wall and towers is the best preserved of the smaller towns of Middle Franconia that have retained their medieval character.

204 ULM. View of the Metzger Tower and the minster from the right bank of the Danube. In the 9th century Ulm was already a Carolingian palatinate and it was raised to the capital town of the duchy of Swabia by the Hohenstaufens in the 12th century. It is situated on the great imperial highway that ran from Flanders to Venice in the Middle Ages and which crosses the Danube highway. Its power and wealth in the 13th and 14th centuries was due to its unique position. Of all the imperial towns, Ulm was the most extensive. The huge task of building the minster was carried out by ten master-builders—largely of two big families: the Parlers from 1377 to 1390, and the Ensingers from 1391 to 1494. The magnificent exterior is the work of the master Matthäus Böblinger between 1447 and 1492. The tower, which is 530 feet high, was completed in 1890 to his designs.

205 LAUINGEN on the Danube. The town stands on the remains of a Roman settlement and in the Late Middle Ages was the seat of the Wittelsbach dukes of Pfalz-Neuburg. The town is dominated by its 180-foot-high tower, begun in 1478, the top part of which was added at the end of the 16th century.

206 INGOLSTADT on the Danube. From 1392 to 1447 it was the residence of the dukes of Bayern-Ingolstadt. Since 1472 it has possessed a university which became a centre of the Roman Catholic Counter-Reformation, more particularly following the establishment of a Jesuit college there in 1555. The town's fortifications are well preserved and the Cross Gate, dating from 1383, is one of the oldest portions. One of the towers of the Late Gothic 'Frauenkirche' dating from the 15th century can be seen in the background.

207 Below DONAUESCHINGEN the River Danube—still near its source—cuts and twists its way between the castles and the chalk rocks of the Swabian hills (Alb). The Augustinian monastery of Beuron grew up here in the 11th century. It was dissolved in 1805 and refounded in 1863 as a Benedictine monastery. In 1868 it was given the status of Benedictine arch-abbacy of Beuron. Parts of the old buildings from the 17th century and the 18th-century chapel are preserved amongst the modern monastery buildings. The new Order is noted for the attention it gives to religious art and music.

208 The BENEDICTINE MONASTERY, WIBLINGEN near Ulm (1099–1806). Its splendid Rococo library dates from the middle of the 18th century.

209 The Benedictine monastery of WELTENBURG on the Danube was founded in 775 by Duke Tassilo III, and was given a new chapel by C. D. Asam between 1717 and 1721. Its simple exterior hides one of the most splendid interiors created by the Bavarian Baroque builders. Our plate shows a view of the chancel, which adjoins the domed, oval nave, and which has been deliberately kept dark so that the figure of St George on the high altar shall assume a visionary appearance.

210 SIGMARINGEN on the Danube is dominated by the castle where the Swabian (Roman Catholic) line of the House of Hohenzollern has resided since 1576. They take their name from Sigmaringen. This huge group of buildings dates from the 12th century and houses an important art collection and a valuable library. It was given its present form after the fire of 1893.

211 PASSAU. View of the Niederhaus, the bishop's castle directly above the confluence of the rivers Ilz and Danube. The old town lies in the triangle between the rivers Inn and Danube, which meet here. It was built on the site of a Roman camp (*Castra Batava*). In 739 it became a bishop's see and its subsequent history has been eventful. Through its many churches and civic buildings—all of which are preserved intact—it has retained the appearance of a large medieval town.

212 WASSERBURG in Upper Bavaria is situated on a narrow tongue of land around which the River Inn flows. The place got its name from a castle which was built in 1087. When the line of the counts of Wasserburg became extinct about 1250, the town became part of Bavaria.

213-14 The old imperial town of REGENSBURG, at the place where the River Regen flows into the Danube, reached the peak of its fortune at the time of the Crusades in the 11th and 12th centuries. About 1180 it was the most densely populated town in Germany, having a favourable situation at the point where the highway from Italy to Central Germany crossed the river highway from the west to Rumania. Many imperial and princely assemblies took place here.

213 The 'GOLDEN TOWER' which dates from the middle of the 13th century. Like the Italian towns (e.g. Bologna), with which many of the Bavarian towns had close connexions, Regensburg also possesses tower residences for the nobility.

214 View of ST PETER'S CATHEDRAL. The old building was destroyed by fire in 1272. The new building was finished in its essentials in the 14th century, but the towers were not completed until 1859.

215-16 AUGSBURG dates from the time of the Roman camp, *Augustra Castra*, which was established in the Rhaetian border province. The town grew rich through trade, first with Italy and later with overseas, especially in the 16th century at the time of the influential merchant families Fugger and Welser.

215 The FUGGEREI, an institution built by Jakob Fugger between 1516 and 1523. In its 52 houses are 106 dwellings. It aptly represents the spirit which prevailed in Augsburg and is a good example of an early communal settlement.

216 Section of the BRONZE DOOR dating from the middle of the 11th century, which today stands in the southern side aisle of the cathedral. The individual panels have designs of Christian or symbolic meaning which were based on ancient originals.

217-19 MUNICH (population 1,033,000) is the capital town of Bavaria and was founded by Henry the Lion in the 12th century. The Wittelsbachs resided here since the 13th century, and it is to them that the town owes most of its important buildings and its fame as a centre of the fine arts.

217 The German Museum for Natural Science and Technology was built 1908-25, at the suggestion of Oskar von Miller.

218 The WITTELSBACH WELL on the Maximiliansplatz, by Adolf Hildebrand, 1895.

219 View from the neo-Gothic Town Hall of the FRAUENKIRCHE, built by Jörg Ganghofer between 1468-88, whose copper-covered towers (of a later date) are a Munich landmark.

220 NYMPHENBURG is one of the earliest palaces Germany owes to Wittelsbachs, who built extensively. It was begun in 1663 by Barelli for the Electress Adelaide. Viscardi added to it in 1702, and it was completed in 1722 by Effner.

221 SCHLEISSHEIM CASTLE near Munich: the new palace was built by the Elector Max Emanuel at the beginning of the 18th century and contains a picture gallery.

222 HOHENSCHWANGEN CASTLE near Füssen, originally called Schwanstein, was rebuilt by Maximilian II in the spirit of the Romantic period.

223 The BENEDICTINE MONASTERY at ETTAL. Founded in 1330 by Emperor Ludwig the Bavarian, it was rebuilt in 1710 to a design by Enrico Zuccalli, and was completed in 1748. The original ground-plan of the central part conformed to the Baroque idea of the use of space and was therefore retained in the new building but was covered by a great dome.

224 OTTOBEUREN. View of the chancel and the southern end of the organ in the monastery church. The choir benches, which are as unique as the building in which they stand, are the work of Martin Herrmann in 1760. The gilded carvings are by J. Christian (cf. Colour Plate VII).

225 The WAGENBRÜCH LAKE, one of the Klaiser Lakes near Mittenwald; on the extreme left the Zugspitze (about 12 miles away) and the Waxenstein; in the distance the Daniel near Ehrwald.

226 Corpus Christi procession in REIT IM WINKEL.

227 At the southern tip of the KÖNIGSEE is the little CHURCH OF ST BARTHOLOMEW, which was built in the first half of the 17th century in the shape of a clover leaf. Behind the church the east face of the Little Watzmann drops sheer to the edge of the lake.

228 View from the Seeköpfel across the SEEALP LAKE and the Oy valley, towards the Nebelhorn (7,340 feet) in the Allgäu Alps.

INDEX

SOURCES OF ILLUSTRATIONS

Erich Angenendt, Ende near Dortmund, 81
Otto Angermayer, Munich, 212, 217, 223, 225, 226
Günther Beyer, Weimar, 143, 182, 185, 189, 190
Albrecht Brugger, Stuttgart-Flughafen, 22, 23
Dr Harald Busch, Frankfurt a. M., 60
Prof. K. H. Clasen, Greifswald, 152
Dähn, Marburg, 62
Deutsche Fotothek, Dresden, 161, 163, 164, 171–173
Deutsche Luftbild K–G, Hamburg, 117, 119
Fritz Eschen, Berlin, 26, 120, 135
Gundermann, Würzburg, 34
Ruth Hallensleben, Wiehl, 75, 76, 77, 79
Hartz-Andres, Hamburg, 118
Robert Häusser, Mannheim, 47, 48
Hehmke-Winterer, Düsseldorf, 27
Heidersberger, Brunswick, 108, 109
Horst Jentsch (Atlantis Verlag), 154
Hans Kenner, Bad König, 28, 31, 149
Gerhard Kerff, 82
Heinz Koberg, Hanover, 105
Henry Koehn, 123
Siegfried Lauterwasser, Überlingen, 3, 4
Photo Marburg, 59
Neukell, Baden-Baden, 103

Alfred Renger-Patzsch, Wameln-Dorf, 80, 83, 84, 102, 130, 157
Hans Retzlaff, Tann, 97, 98, 169
Fritz Rotgans, Duisburg, 51, 75
Hans Saebens, Worpswede, 6, 36, 57, 86–95, 107, 115, 122, 124, 162, 165–8
Helga Schmidt-Glassner, Stuttgart, 29, 30, 58, 101, 150, 179
Toni Schneiders, Lindau, III, 8, 11, 39, 85, 106, 114, 116, 121, 125–129, 136, 137, 140, 208, 222
Ludwig Schuster, Munich, 194, 218, 219, 220, 221, 223, 227, 228
Staatliche Bildstelle, Berlin, 153
Photo Stober, Freiburg i. Br., 17
Photo Volkswagenwerk, Wolfsburg, 104
Widmann, 170
Dr Wolff & Tritschler, Frankfurt a. M., 65, 67

Plates 96, 151, and 174 are in the archives of Atlantis Verlag, Zurich; all the rest not credited to other sources were taken by the editor. The publishers wish to express their gratitude to all the photographers for their kind co-operation.